It Means the World to Us

CHESHIRE PRIZE FOR LITERATURE ANTHOLOGIES

Prize Flights: Stories from the Cheshire Prize for Literature 2003; edited by **Ashley Chantler**

Life Lines: Poems from the Cheshire Prize for Literature 2004; edited by **Ashley Chantler**

Word Weaving: Stories and Poems for Children from the Cheshire Prize for Literature 2005; edited by **Jaki Brien**

Edge Words: Stories from the Cheshire Prize for Literature 2006; edited by **Peter Blair**

Elements: Poems from the Cheshire Prize for Literature 2007; edited by **Peter Blair**

Wordscapes: Stories and Poems for Children from the Cheshire Prize for Literature 2008; edited by **Jaki Brien**

Zoo: Short Stories from the Cheshire Prize for Literature 2009; edited by **Emma L. E. Rees**

Still Life: Poetry from the Cheshire Prize for Literature 2010; edited by **Emma L. E. Rees**

Wordlife: Stories and Poems for Children from the Cheshire Prize for Literature 2011; edited by **Jaki Brien**

Lost and Found: Short Stories from the Cheshire Prize for Literature 2012; edited by **Emma L. E. Rees**

Great Escapes: Poetry from the Cheshire Prize for Literature 2013; edited by **Emma L. E. Rees**

Out of this Word: Stories and Poems for Children from the Cheshire Prize for Literature 2014; edited by **Jaki Brien**

Patches of Light: Short Stories from the Cheshire Prize for Literature 2015; edited by **Ian Seed**

Crossings Over: Poetry from the Cheshire Prize for Literature 2016; edited by **Ian Seed**

Opening Words: Stories and Poems for Children from the Cheshire Prize for Literature 2017; edited by **Simon E. Poole**

Island Chain: Short Stories from the Cheshire Prize for Literature 2018; edited by **William Stephenson**

Unlocked: Writing from the Cheshire Prize for Literature 2020; edited by **Simon E. Poole and William Stephenson**

It Means the World to Us

Writing from the
Cheshire Prize for Literature 2021

Edited by
Simon E. Poole
and Harry Parkin

University of Chester Press

First published 2022
by University of Chester Press
Parkgate Road
Chester CH1 4BJ

Printed and bound in the UK by the
LIS Print Unit
University of Chester
Cover designed by the LIS Graphics Team
University of Chester

This collection © University of Chester, 2022
Individual contributions © their respective authors

The right of Simon E. Poole and Harry Parkin to be identified as the joint editors of this work have been asserted in accordance with the Copyright, Designs and Patents Act 1988

The moral rights of the contributors to be identified as the authors of this work have been asserted in accordance with the Copyright, Designs and Patents Act 1988

All Rights Reserved
No part of this publication may be reproduced, stored in a retrieval system or transmitted in any form or by any means without the prior permission of the copyright owner, other than as permitted by UK copyright legislation or under the terms and conditions of a recognised copyright licensing scheme

A catalogue record of this book is available
from the British Library

ISBN 978-1-910481-18-9

CONTENTS

Contributors	vii
Foreword	xiv
The World Needs Everyone's Help **Emily Simpson**	1
Things I Liked About Our Planet **Esme Alice Blue**	2
Bless Earth **Sophia Morris-Jones**	3
A Letter to Earth **Aurora B. Blue**	4
Miracles **Daniel Johnson**	6
The Breadfruit Bone **Connor Johnston**	8
One, Two, Tree **Ella Catherine Barrett**	9
The Nature Dragon **Maia Russell**	12
What the World Once Was **Eva Mallouris**	15
Often **Dannielle Jones**	17

It Means the World to Us

This Cat Grows Old **Molly Nash**	18
The Absence of Stars **Yvonne Taylor**	21
The Monster Who Moved to Ecotown **Eleanor Cullen**	26
Willow **Laura Hall**	31
Marsha's Plan to Save the Sea **Jenna Thirtle**	34
Pale Blue Dot **Philip Williams**	39
Duir **Helen Kay**	41
Interview **Cathy Bryant**	42
Salvaged **Eve Naden**	48
Awareness **Beth Westbrook**	53
The Apple **Ben Saunders**	69

CONTRIBUTORS

Ella Catherine Barrett has a deep love of stories and storytelling, enjoying everything from *A Hundred and One Dalmatians*, to Harry Potter, to *Hamlet* (albeit in abridged form!). She wrote and illustrated her story *One, Two, Tree* aged seven, intending to do nothing more than share it with close family and friends. After everyone's glowing feedback, however, she decided to enter it for the Cheshire Prize for Literature. She's very glad she did!

Aurora B. Blue has lived in Cheshire East for 11 years and has been writing for contests and publication since 2017, with a commended poem 'Fantastic Plastic Winter' at the Buxton Literary Festival. She was runner up in the Ted Hughes/Elmet prize in 2018 and won the Ledbury Prize for under 11s that year, too; she won, again, first prize at Ledbury in 2019, with 'The Cat that Nobody Wanted'; and came first in 2021 in the Writing East Midlands prize, with her poem, 'The Moor Reclaims'. Aurora has been a co-editor of *The Outlaw* magazine for The Arthur Ransome Society, the journal for junior members for several years. She enjoys writing haiku and has co-written and co-produced a book of haiku which is sold to fund donations to MSF. Aurora spends her non-writing time making art, for which she has been awarded several winning honours over the years. She enjoys mountaineering all around the UK and Ireland.

It Means the World to Us

Esme Alice Blue is a keen artist and photographer. This year she won first prize for under 21s in the Derbyshire Open Art competition for her Music of the Woods 3D origami sculpture; she scooped several honours at the local Allotment and Gardens Association show – first, second and third in photography; first for a Miniature Garden; first for her sunflower art and won a special cup! She has had her photography recognised at the Shepton Mallet Snowdrop Festival; she was longlisted on the Young Poets Network for her poem, 'Ode to 30 Cows' in 2020; she was a winning poet at the 2021 IF Oxford: The Oxford Science and Ideas Festival with 'How to Grow an Apple Tree'; and she has had a number of haiku feature on the Japan Society website Haiku Corner. Esme also co-writes for *The Outlaw* magazine for The Arthur Ransome Society. Esme adores animals and cares for three guinea pigs. She also mountaineers and has scaled all of the three highest UK peaks, plus a Munro or so! Esme is home educated.

Cathy Bryant was homeless in her teens and then worked as a life model, shoe shop assistant, civil servant and childminder. When she became too disabled to work full time, Cathy started submitting her writing. She has now had hundreds of pieces published all over the world (six continents!) and three poetry collections, as well as having won over 30 literary awards, including the Bulwer-Lytton Fiction Prize and the Wergle Flomp Award for Humorous Poetry, plus the Cheshire Prize for Literature (twice). Cathy's latest poetry collection is *Erratics*, from Arachne Press, and her bestselling book is *How to Win Writing Competitions*. Cathy also runs the Comps and Calls website that lists free opportunities for writers every month. She lives in Salford, UK, with her husband, who is a bestselling writer in his own right.

Contributors

Eleanor Cullen grew up in New Brighton and lets her love for seaside towns influence everything she writes. She has a BA degree in English Literature and Creative Writing and an MA in Screenwriting, but her greatest achievement is bringing up her canine writing companion Harley. Her debut children's book was published in 2021, and since then she has written numerous children's poems and stories. Being a winner of the Cheshire Prize for Literature means the absolute world to her! And, along with Harley, she can't wait to hear readers' reactions to 'The Monster Who Moved to Ecotown'.

Laura Hall is a writer and journalist who grew up in Stockport and now lives in Copenhagen. She has a deep fascination with wildness and wild people. She has been shortlisted in multiple writing competitions, including the BBC World Service International Radio Playwriting competition; she is delighted to have finally taken the top spot. Laura is also the author of *One Day, So Many Ways*, a children's book about how life is lived around the world, along with *Time Out Copenhagen* and a range of other travel titles. She is currently deep into a project about wild swimming in Scandinavia and has further plans to write short stories for children with a wild and untameable heart.

Daniel Johnson grew up in Cheshire and was an avid reader from an early age. As he grew up, daydreams gradually turned into poetry, and he is now studying at a local college while still writing poetry when an idea comes to mind. He enjoys expressing emotion and important feelings through poetry and is also enjoying developing his work.

It Means the World to Us

Connor Johnston grew up on the Wirral and studied English and French Literature at the University of Oxford, where he won the Lord Alfred Douglas Prize for a sonnet written under lockdown. He is currently teaching English as a foreign language in Lille and hopes to be a published novelist one day.

Dannielle Jones is a 14- (almost 15-) year-old writer, who is growing up in a small community just outside of Chester. She attends school, writes for a Young Writers' company, and wishes to attend one of the top universities in the UK – Oxford. In her spare time, away from writing, Dannielle can be found playing badminton, or video games. Her cat, Pip, and late fish, Blue, continue to be her two greatest inspirations.

Helen Kay is from Nantwich. Her pamphlet, *This Lexia & Other Languages* (V. Press) was born in 2020. She curates the Poetry Dyslexia and Imagination project supporting writing about learning differences. Helen is known on social media for her diva hen puppet, Nigella. In 2021 she was a finalist for the Brotherton Prize.

Eva Mallouris comes from a Cypriot background and lives in Widnes. She loves reading and writing and is very passionate about different causes around the world. She loves Arabic cuisine and would always be enthusiastic about attending a poetry slam. Eva's favourite authors/poets are Rupi Kaur, followed by Elizabeth Acevedo and Mahogany L. Brown, and she loves the singer Faousia.

Contributors

Sophia Morris-Jones enjoys playing football, swimming, acting, singing, dancing, and playing the piano when she isn't writing poetry! Sophia is passionate about the environment and protecting the natural world, particularly the oceans. When visiting the beach, she can often be seen picking up litter in between building sandcastles and having a paddle! Sophia lives with her parents and younger sister in Cheshire.

Yvette (Eve) Naden writes everything from wacky poetry to disturbing short stories and is currently working on a novel about philosophical robots. She was born in France, but now resides in the UK, and currently attends the University of York. Her work has featured in *The Roadrunner Review*, The Elmbridge Literary Competition publication and, in 2021, she won the Zealous Short Story Competition. When she isn't writing, she can be found thinking about writing or reading overdue library books.

Molly Nash was born in Wirral and, as of yet, her favourite adventures have been her ambitions as she embarks on her journey as a writer. She is studying English Literature and History, hoping to make her mark on both as she scrawls away in every medium she can. Her favourite form of writing is performative poetry, and the Cheshire Prize provides a fantastic platform for this. Her biggest inspiration is the night sky – it has been around for so long – how many lives the stars must have seen!

Maia Russell is nine years old and was born on Halloween. This is why she likes lots of Halloween stuff like bats and cats. Her favourite fruit is a lemon, and her favourite TV show is *Ghosts*. She also likes space and galaxy stuff because she was named after a star.

It Means the World to Us

Ben Saunders writes plays and stories which intertwine everyday characters with out of the ordinary situations. He studied Natural Sciences and Psychology at Durham University, before gaining a PhD in the Psychology of Discourse from the University of Manchester. He lived in Cheshire before moving to Manchester where he currently lives with his family. His first novel, *Senescence: The Ashes of Youth* is now available on Amazon and trade paperback from T Rex books.

Emily Simpson is seven years old and lives in Manchester with her family. She loves playing football, collecting toy bunnies and being creative. This was her first competition, and she is delighted that her poem was chosen as a winning entry.

Yvonne Taylor is originally from Macclesfield, and now lives in a Victorian seaside town on the south coast of Wales. She lives with her husband and two children, James and Ben. James is 10 and has a kicky-up record of 233. Ben is seven and would like to change his name to Bob in time for his eighth birthday. In between work and ferrying the boys to football matches, Yvonne loves to write short stories. Her kicky-up record is five – she's promised to keep trying.

Jenna Thirtle is a recent University of Chester English Language graduate. Moving to Chester after a year of teaching in Spain she picked up a passion for writing children's stories whilst living abroad. This is her first entry into any writing competition and she is honoured to have been shortlisted.

Contributors

Beth Westbrook is a neurodivergent actor/writer with chronic pain from The Wirral. She started writing as part of SalFUNNI 2018, the first cohort of students from the University of Salford who went up to write and perform at the Edinburgh Fringe. She was longlisted for a Funny Women Writing Award in 2019, a finalist for Hope Mill's Through the Mill Prize in 2021, shortlisted for the 2021 Women's Prize for Playwriting, and is well chuffed to have won a Cheshire Prize for Literature. Improving the representation of neurodiversity is hugely important to Beth. She is also a Pisces who would love to write for *Doctor Who* one day so if you have access to the TARDIS hook her up!

Philip Williams is spread thinly across the Cheshire Plain. He has lived in Alsager since 2007 and for his sins is involved with local and regional politics at town and borough level. He grew up in South Wales, spent two years in Australia as a 'Ten Pound Pom' in the '60s and studied English at Leeds University in the 1980s. He has worked in marketing, publicity and marketing research. His poems have appeared in *Agenda*, *Iota*, *Tears in the Fence*, *Planet*, *Poetry Wales* and regional anthologies. He previously won the Cheshire Prize for poetry in 2013. He is widowed with two grown-up daughters and is active on the regional poetry scene.

FOREWORD

Do you know it was the inkcap mushroom that I first thought of when I came to write the editorial to this superb collection of works?! That probably sounds strange or odd, but as I contemplated the meaning of sustainability, I was drawn, perhaps inevitably, like many of the authors herein, towards one's own connection with nature, and the metaphors that encapsulate that connection.

I often find myself writing about nature anyway but in this instance, for me, the rumination immediately took me back to a poem entitled 'Shiro', that I wrote some years ago, about the bizarre way the inkcap's spores are spread: through the ink of the mushroom no less; google 'deliquesce' if you're interested!

Needless to say, I certainly was, because it represented something to me about the link between our own identity and our community's identity; between nature and time, and particularly how we feel about these links: their verdant vibration, cycling, recycling, turning around seasonally like one of the Greek understandings of time. Not the linear march of time, that we commonly think of, and so readily connect with the notion of progress, but the cyclical time of Aion, revolving, and deeply, even religiously resonating with us; like our ancestors.

I suppose in some ways this understanding of time is why tradition has always fascinated me. But, I don't mean the curator-style understanding of tradition; I mean the kind that wrestles with innovation: so that we can somehow arrive in a perpetuity that uses progress as a means of achieving a sustainable and harmonious existence with our planet; not a use of chronological progress that correlates with more and bigger things or becoming

Foreword

richer or greater, all of which ultimately leads to depletion, the exploitation of resources and the desolation of nature.

As I've mentioned, many authors did write about nature. So, I can't resist another connection with Greek here. The connection in the etymology of 'anthology', originally also from Greek 'anthologia'; from *anthos* meaning 'flower', and *-logia* meaning 'collection' or 'study'. In Greek, the word originally denoted a collection of 'flowers' of verse, small choice poems or epigrams, by different authors.

Well, this collection of flowers most definitely deals with sustainability in a way that is often positive, optimistic, dare I say 'hopeful'? Many of the single specimens offer a solution or warning of how simple actions can contribute to making a more content eternity, can become cultural traditions that innovate, or can offer a possible way of living which marries the notions of progress with sustainability, and deepens our sense of place in nature. A marriage between Chronos and Aion perhaps, a combination that brings Kairos to the fore, the third Greek god of time. A marriage that is felt through what I call be-longing, which rather than representing a past full of poor judgements, leading to a precarious present and the hope of a sustainable future, instead represents the feeling that this is the opportune moment to act and create a more stable and cyclic, unbounded existence for us all.

Shiro

I am a spore,
a growing hypha.
Reaching out.
Attempting to connect.
Seeking community.

It Means the World to Us

Just as homokaryotic
mycelium,
exist only to find
other mycelium
of the same ilk.
Through this earth
we call home.
We join.
Become dikaryotic.
Hope for a fruiting body
with its own identity.
Which, existing within
A circle, a ring,
recognises the tension between
its identity and community:
Each compromising the other;
Each must give way if the other
Is to exist;
Each erodes the other.
We must dark
and deliquesce
from the lower edge.
Decompose ourselves,
to drip a new spore through ink,
to face the same dilemma.
Knowing that,
eventually,
each of us will be
just a stipe
with a very small black disc
perched on top.

Foreword

I would like to thank the judges for playing such an important part in making this competition such a success, to the entrants whose creativity never fails to inspire us, to colleagues at Storyhouse and the University for their contributions and to everyone who continues to support the Cheshire Prize for Literature in the wider community. The competition and resulting anthology reflect the key importance of culture in bringing people together for the benefit of society – it really does mean the world to us.

Si Poole
Associate Professor of Cultural Education and
Senior Lead of Cultural Education and Research
at Storyhouse

THE WORLD NEEDS EVERYONE'S HELP

Emily Simpson

Poetry category for 4–7 years

Trees are falling to the ground
which means pandas can't eat their bamboo right now.
Polar bears are getting too hot
because of global warming the ice is melting, all the lot.
If you drop trash on the floor
you could make animals sick, that's for sure.
So now let's help the planet all forever
so we can be fit and stay together!

THINGS I LIKED ABOUT OUR PLANET

Esme Alice Blue

Poetry category for 8–10 years

The beauty of the wild world was
rainbows of birdsong,
pinks of roses,
redness of foxes,
the heartbeat of winds,
the sharp shark teeth of waves in the seas,
long, wavy grasses around the mountains
all cooled and warmed by winds
as damp as soil or as dry as dead leaves
and every part was a piece of the same jigsaw.

BLESS EARTH

Sophia Morris-Jones

Poetry category for 8–10 years

Bless Earth

Give our planet what it needs,
Pick up litter,
Plant trees,
Bless Earth.

Look after our world,
Make sure it's healthy,
Appreciate living on this planet,
It is our precious home we inhabit,
Bless Earth.

Try not to use too much electricity,
Because that's not good for the planet, you see,
Do not recklessly devour Earth's gifts,
Reuse, recycle, repair, reduce,
Don't let our planet be abused,
Bless Earth.

The leaves that grow,
Give us oxygen to breathe,
Nature's warning signs we must heed,
Time is ticking, there is more to be done,
Let's work together sustainably,
And finish the job that we have begun,
Bless Earth.

A LETTER TO EARTH

Aurora B. Blue

Poetry category for 11–13 years

In spite of this cutting   stealing   greying   meaningless
    choking choke
of burning trees and habitats and lives
    I see that EARTH is beautiful still – so Earth awake!
    I hear a murmur, a rumour spreading through the
        bleakness of masses like me;
it is filled with SURVIVAL THRIVING BLOOMING
    GREENNESSES
and a still proud flesh swelling my heart beats free,
freely as the one-hearted pulse of the world.
    I am witness to windswept links
    between humidities and droughts –
    I think long about airborne diseases.
I sing a lamentation to scorched
lands and pot-bellied floods,
to invisible toxic airs and societies' scars of
greed-patterned scarcities
where clean matter burns: leaving lands barren
whose scarred sounds fall silent on cues;
ravens and curlews,
barred in invisible bands of electro – magnetic hues
beneath the brain-baking sun
(Bringer of Life and Death), call that the strike of the gong has begun,

A Letter to Earth

beating down in a recurring dream:
    spinning in my sleep, everything is perfect, not
        burning –
where peaceful surrounds peace surrounds us
deathless, warless, wordless, hungerless,
where all-coloured birds sing freely, truly, clearly;
    but awake now, still-wet lungs breathe seeds of death
and skulls burn inside out,
as I learn that resistance is hidden
behind forbidden faces
blinded by their own lines of flight,
and a new scarceness revives new lies;
chatter is wound into tight knots of silence,
bound with in-rules.
An essence of foxyness is drowned alongside truths:
Warning: love was forbidden, togetherness
    banished;
snug powerful towers were disguised and more life died,
frazzled from lack of water and suchlike,
as humidity sucked away smugly,
and moods changed as minds changed and
    everything changed
as trust disappeared.
But then again –

growing into depths
shooting through the soiled ground
faintly colours burst.

MIRACLES

Daniel Johnson

Poetry category for 17–18 years

I dream, and the view outside,
Does not look so green anymore.
I dream, and see food shortages in the shops,
And wildfires on the news.
I dream, and I walk through a park,
That feels alien to me now.

I dream that I drive,
To familiar places tainted.
I dream of the heat on my skin,
Dryness on my lips and the aching in my brain.
I take a walk where I left my heart,
But all I feel are tears.
I dream of my home, but it is not as I knew.

I dream, restless now,
Of people displaced and fighting in the streets.
I dream of the sea advancing and the heavens opening,
Waves lashing and rivers bursting.

Dream twists into nightmare,
As smoke rises on the horizon.
Mass graves follow mass migration
And rain turns acidic on my skin.
The air in my lungs turns sour, and

Miracles

I awaken with a start, and gasp for air.
I blink tears from my eyes,
And stare at the blank ceiling.
I wish to return to my childhood,
Fresh air and unscarred lungs,
A life not cut short by the air I breathe.

I turn over in my hospital bed.
I am too old to believe in miracles.

THE BREADFRUIT BONE

Connor Johnston

Poetry category for 19–24 years

Breadfruit makes for funky food but twists my stomach knotted.
Apples leave me empty as if all our middles rotted,
Fig trees burst the terracotta pots in which they're potted,
Long and thick bananas always seem by blackness spotted,
I could pulp a pomegranate, claim to be exotic,
But I won't eat the ruby fruit, nor thumb a peach, nor prod it,
I might've sniffed the mangled mush, and in its fumes besotted,
I could have tasted wondrous things and since that night forgot it,
I could have wandered far and wide and all the green globe trotted,
I could have made a mushroom house and stayed a while or squatted,
I could have grown a thousand trees and with their roots complotted
To wriggle through the concrete floors and concrete lords garrotted,
But I don't have the breadfruit bone, I simply haven't got it!
And yet I watch it brown and wilt, this lot I've been allotted.

ONE, TWO, TREE

Ella Catherine Barrett

Short story category for 4–7 years

It was a warm, sunny day and it was especially sunny in one bit of woodland and in this magical woodland there was a tree. There were lots of trees of course but this one was special because in this tree was a squirrel treehouse (a very small treehouse fit for a squirrel in case you were wondering).

In this treehouse there lived a rather small but happy family. There was a mother squirrel, a father squirrel and three baby squirrels. The baby squirrels' names were Toto the youngest, Pompom the oldest and Fluffy the one in the middle. Toto is shy and only opens up to her friends. Pompom likes adventure and daydreaming. Fluffy is the logical one and very clever.

The babies were starting to whine about food but their mother said it was not time for her to go hunting yet and she would go in a minute if they were patient. And so, they waited and daydreamed and thought and talked for a minute or two. Finally, their mother hopped down the tree to go hunt (for nuts) while their father was busy making sure that even super, super strong wind could not make a hole or a dent in their treehouse.

It was not long before their mother had scurried out of sight that the squirrels heard the most terrifying noise a squirrel can hear. The noise of a chainsaw and it was getting louder and louder and closer and closer until the tree gave a wobble and another and another until

… CRASH the whole tree had come very close to being totally destroyed but the same was not to say for the treehouse. It was

It Means the World to Us

totally destroyed and so was their dad. The children had jumped off just in time but their dad just wasn't fast enough. And so, they all waited for their mother to come back and when she found out about their dad she wept for a while but eventually when she stopped they packed up their nuts and went to a different forest.

When they got there, they found a nice tree and started to build another treehouse. After a while they met a fox. They were scared at first but the fox promised them no harm. Then she introduced herself.

"I wish you no harm. Oh, and by the way please call me Professor Mcfoxy," whispered Professor Mcfoxy.

"I'm Toto," squeaked Toto shyly.

"I'm Pompom and this is Fluffy. By the way why are you whispering?" shouted Pompom.

"I dunno," answered the Professor. "I like this tree too well under it really but yeah," she yowled.

"We shall tell you are [our] story of woe," said Fluffy and so they did. At the end the Professor said "I think I might know who cut down your tree."

"Oh tell us please," begged the squirrels.

"Okay then," said the fox. "I think it was my arch enemy Evil Enemy. His ancestors have been cutting down trees for centuries," she said wisely. "If you want me to, I can adventure out and investigate," she said.

"Oh yes please," they all said together.

"OK then," she said and she set off.

She worked her way through the forest and after a while she got thirsty. "I should have brought some water," she thought. "Well never mind I'm sure to find a pond or something soon," she thought. And soon she did and the water looked black but when she got closer she found it was the reflection of Evil Enemy's lair.

One, Two, Tree

Finally, she had found it. Now she only needed to find him and put him in the indestructible prison and help the squirrels build their treehouse.

So, she went to go and climb the crumbly wall that surrounded the scary lair.

When she got over the wobbly wall she went closer to the horrible house and saw Evil Enemy through the window. "I bet I can climb through that window that is open," thought the Professor and she did and then she got out some knock-out drops and when Evil Enemy smelt them he fell into a deep sleep.

"Now I need to call my deer friends to help me lift him," she whispered and she did. All her deer friends came and helped her lift him into the indestructible prison. Then she found her way back to the squirrels and helped them.

THE NATURE DRAGON

Maia Russell

Short story category for 8–10 years

The truth is it's actually a dragon.

You see this dragon was sent to earth after the dinosaurs. They had a different dragon back then. Under the dragon lies treasures like diamond, platinum, emeralds, rubies and gold. You name it, it was there. Below all that is the lava core of the earth. The dragon breathed that itself. But on the surface was all the greenery or what had meant to be greenery.

The dragon loved all her forests, woods and meadows but the one she loved the most was Fairy Forest. And once there was a man called Victor. He was born in 1819 though this story is set in 2889. But when he was 70 he found a witch's cabin. It had shelves of all different potions for all different effects. But this wasn't the nice man you'd see walking around the local shop getting a present for someone else. No. This man just wanted to get the best most powerful potion there was. The immortal potion. As he greedily swiped the potion off the ancient, wooden and run-down shelf he grew a cheeky grin and ran quickly back to his incredibly posh home. He sat at his glass table and rambunctiously slurped it down.

Finally, the story begins: 2889
Victor had set up an infamous logging company called Victor's Nature Destroyer. He set it up when a man called Richard Louis invented the Auto Logger. As soon as Victor heard he rushed to the shops to get his hands on some, but it was £7,000. Which was

The Nature Dragon

not a problem for Victor since he was already rich. He then had a nefarious scheme. He would set up a logging company. All his workers were as corrupt as him. Always in it for money. He evilly handed each an Auto Logger and everyone got to work until they had cut down every forest apart from the Fairy Forest.

Legend had it that when people were still using axes they had attempted to cut down a tree from that place but the dragon arose like the Lorax and started to attack. But did Victor care about legends? No. All he'd ever cared about was his money. Also the Auto Logger could wipe out an entire forest in one go. So he'd be fine. Right? He paid his workers and told them all about it. He told them that he'd need backup if the legend was real, to overcome the mighty beast. So, they packed their bags and set off to Snowdonia where Fairy Forest lay.

When they arrived, Victor unloaded his Auto Logger and cast it over the last forest. All the trees fell to the ground. The workers started to suffer. Everyone in the world actually. All apart from Victor and all because of Victor. Suddenly he knew why. In the 2010s and 2020s there were people chanting "Trees = Oxygen". He knew what he'd done and felt surprisingly guilty. This was really strange for someone with such a cold heart. But he knew that according to legend he would have to fight the dragon. Apprehension waved through him. Suddenly the furious head of the enraged dragon emerged from the ground, ready for battle.

"Help!" Victor screamed before realising that he was all alone. He thought quickly. "Right, if this is an eco-dragon then its weakness must be plastic!"

He rummaged through his satchel and found a bunch of plastic. He tossed it at the dragon and it groaned a sigh of pain. Once the dragon had regained its strength it breathed a ball of

It Means the World to Us

magma at Victor. He realised that the dragon was unbeatable and admitted that he'd lost. He sat down, defeated. The dragon then realised that Victor was sorry for everything he'd done and gave humans a second chance. The dragon used its magic to regenerate all the forests, plants and animals (including humans). The workers came back and the dragon returned all the humans' technology and houses, but this time they were all eco-friendly.

WHAT THE WORLD ONCE WAS

Eva Mallouris

Short story category for 11–13 years

Next is a replica of a tree. See the branches? Like angels' arms reaching to God. See the leaves? Emeralds in the streetlights. With roots to every land and intertwined in the soft soil. Soil like silk. It gives birth to the flowers and gives life to the trees.

Following on, we have the sky. I doubt anyone has seen it through the smog. Home to flecks of gold, silver and every colour imaginable. An abyss of clustering flames. Then there is the sun and moon both bright and towering. Queens of their own skies for how could they own the same heavens? The simple way to describe the sky is as a diamond hourglass.

In these skies lived birds like we have today but gleaming with resplendence. They wore haloes. Ours are grey and dull but theirs had magic. They could become clouds dipping in and out of paradise. Flowing like wisps of rain it silences the thunder.

In the past there were large areas of glorious, pure life. Everything was alive, the colours and species were artwork on a clear canvas. Liberty never rested as it ran with the squirrels and crept with the ivy and swung with the monkeys. Raindrops could spill from leaves making them jewels. The sweet fruits were vibrant blessings and the cool air stung on their face. Verdant and vivid the canopies draped down stroking the heads of terrified flowers as they saw the machines approaching.

Finally, we have the ocean. You can't describe it with words. Like glass the way it bites your skin. Sharp as the wind, blooming with life and glowing with colours. It was like rosewater and

It Means the World to Us

lemon juice and honey and tears all in one. In it were dolphins, radiating with freedom and fish of the galaxy: choking. The ocean led to the beach which was a place of relaxation. Warm sand ran through your fingers and Aphrodite's foam dancing lightly on your skin.

    I hope you enjoyed this tour. Tickets are now available to see the most realistic replica of animals such as polar bears, rhinos, tigers and an orangutan so if you're interested be sure to check it out. Thank you for visiting the museum of The Old Mother Earth.

OFTEN

Dannielle Jones

Poetry category for 14–16 years

I often think back to when I was young, Reminisce on the times when I didn't have the constant, Bitter bites of mankind's action everywhere, Surrounding me, Engulfing me.

I like to think that it's my problem, in this sick reality, The news articles I read, The videos I listen to on repeat, The radio man who just blames everybody but himself. I try and do my part, I genuinely do, Try and make a change, But often I find no difference, Instead, an urge to give up.

They say, *'A small difference leads to a big difference'* But when you actually think about, No naivety, No childlike visions,

Does it really?
Or will it take the whole world to make one change?
One world, or one man?

I often recall hearing nothing about our dying world, Nothing about Climate Change, Nothing about War, Nothing about Sustainability, trying to make a change,

But at the end of the day, This is *our* world.

Who else is going to make a change if not me and you and the youth?

I often recall fixating on death, The death of the Arctic, The death of the Globe,

And these articles would come out, Over and over again, But did that reporter care, I ask you as a person, Did he?

Or is *'his part'* using paper from dying forests to complete his job and get paid?

THIS CAT GROWS OLD

Molly Nash

Short story category for 11–13 years

A chance.

But it was already too late.

Aiming for a rooftop, Auden leapt gracefully, fumbled on her comically large paws, and launched herself into a gutter. Embarrassed, she checked over her shoulder. A pigeon was studying her, studiously.

She glared at it, glarefully, and it shot into the sky like a surprise.

Recovering from her disastrous attempt to be a Cat, Auden caught sight of a newspaper. It was slowly making the transition from paper to mulch as the rain sank its tendrils in the ink.

'*The Herald*', it read. Glaswegian, interesting.

Beneath the impromptu chromatography test, an offensively bold headline blared 'COP26' and, originally, nothing else. Below *that*, half a sentence that *may* have ended 'global warming', but could have as easily been 'snowfall warning' or, Auden hoped, flicking her tail, 'goats are swarming' steadily merged into the next line.

Sadly, she reasoned that a cohort of hollow-horned mammals was *not* newsworthy and settled on the first.

The proper term was 'Climate Change', anyway.
It didn't matter in the grand scheme of things. Certainly not to Auden. But it was intrinsically human to bicker over the colour of the flame rather than douse the fire.

Or to use the fire escape.

This Cat Grows Old

Dying didn't scare the kitten, just as it hadn't scared the cats before her. The only issue was, she quite liked the world.

Even if it *was* full of idiots and tyrants and people who liked Marmite on toast.

Because the majority of people were fine. Very few were definitively good, because very few were definitively wicked. *Most* were just human. Bad luck, she supposed, wandering along the slate roofs.

An open window distracted her. Or rather, the noise from *within* the open window distracted her – a voice stalked her ear from behind prodded at her brain relentlessly until Auden *listened* to it. Not heard it, *listened* to it.

Young as it was, it was so heavy with passion that Auden was surprised when it was able to lilt upwards as sentences rolled to a close.

"– the science has been crystal clear. How dare you continue to look away and come here saying that you're doing enough, when the politics and solutions needed are still nowhere in sight –"

The voice was angry now, heat radiating from a young girl projected in the television, face contorted with grief and desperation and rage, breaking over Auden in waves of … was it hope?

It couldn't be – she didn't *care* about humans.

They were big and stupid and careless; they took solace only in the weight of their pockets and the temperature of their bath. They paid attention to things that didn't matter, the way a fictional character spoke or looked or acted, and didn't give a passing thought to the children starving on the streets. Humans barely cared about those around them. Not the people of yesterday, or the unlucky fools of tomorrow.

Why should Auden care if they drove themselves to extinction? It was their own fault.

It Means the World to Us

But as declarations and insults and vows cascaded from the pixels, they washed over the kitten in fierce promises of hope; a molten panacea coursed through her veins, reaching her eyes and her heart and her paws four times too large. It poked at her stoic nonchalance, hammered at the door of her ignorance, scowled and glowered and glared with shame at Auden's acceptance of the end.

One more life. Twenty years, if she was lucky. Perhaps (and Auden hated herself for hoping) they could change, they could fix this God-forsaken calamity forsaken, not by God, but His children.

The next generation had a chance with passion like this, fury directed at all the right people.

A deep brogue drowned out the girl's pleading.

"What time is she arriving then?"

And another, slightly lighter voice, bellowed back, "Fifteen minutes! Fancy wandering down?"

She was coming here? Well then.

Auden had nothing else to do, after all, and seeing humans sort out their issues was always … actually, come to think of it, she hadn't seen it before.

She could make a day trip of it.

All cats, throughout history, have found themselves delighted in human suffering. All except one.

So, if she happened to care about the oafs, was it really the end of the world?

Pattering down a cobbled street, a kitten envisioned a future led by a generation she could grow old with. A generation that demanded without shame, helped without coercion. A generation that *cared*.

No.

Perhaps it wasn't the end of the world at all.

THE ABSENCE OF STARS

Yvonne Taylor

Short story category for 25+ years

Footsteps. After countless miles even the soft, dusty land is merciless, unrelenting. I glance over my shoulder at the ground behind me, expecting to see evidence of the agony I feel – smouldering embers in the dust, sharp thorns adorned with glistening droplets of blood. But there's nothing except faint footprints. No evidence of suffering, or even our existence. Like ants we continue, with purpose but with our destination, and our fate, unknown. Mama's dress gently swooshes and swirls with each footstep, the hypnotic movement of its bold pattern mesmerising.

I think of the home we've left behind, now out of reach, perhaps forever. The rippling lake with all its glorious treasures. Long, magical days exploring every part of its water, armed with nothing but a stick. Gently prodding, poking, lifting, looking – learning about all the life it contained, each creature as magnificent and intriguing as the next. Beautiful patterns, strange movements, a myriad of colours.

There have been no lakes along our journey. Like our hometown, the waters receded, and the once luscious, leafy crops vanished – all that remains is barren land devoid of meaningful life. The occasional carcass of an unfortunate animal can be found as we traverse the amber terrain. Some of the people pick through the putrid remains for grubs and bugs that might offer some tiny morsels of nutrition. The empty land offers no opportunity for respite or shelter from the sun that blisters and burns through the angry, auburn sky. The beautiful sound of leaves rustling in the wind, small creatures chirruping and chirping, gleeful shrieks of playing children are no more. We stumble upon the occasional hut, but all so far have been deserted, their occupants long gone. We should have left sooner. Dada said so.

I feel the threatening tingling of tears in my face, but the drought appears to have hit me as well as our land. I know better than to sob.

Mama walks before me, BeBe on her hip. Her once glowing skin is bruised, blistered and encrusted with dirt. Despite her youth, her shoulders are hunched from carrying poor, patient BeBe for so long. I wonder what he will remember, his eyes seeing this desolate world afresh. I dream of asking Mama if we're nearly there yet, wishing the answer would be yes. Longing to see some signs of hope or mercy.

I try to block out the pain with memories of the stars. Their twinkling beauty, their fascinating shapes and patterns serenely punctuating the vast expanse of magnificent inky sky. How I hope to gaze at them again – to be cradled in my Mama's arms, nestled on warm earth beneath a translucent sky. I see Dada's face. Oh, how I miss his gentle hands, his warm smile, the way he made Mama laugh like a child. My fingers have traced the deep lines and furrows on the map of his face a million times over – I know them as well as the patterns of the stars. 'Hard work', he called them. Sometimes I draw those lines in the dust, hoping it will cast a mysterious spell and bring him back to me, with all of the other things I sorely miss.

"Effy, what are you doing?" Mama asks softly. "Just drawing, Mama." I can't bear to tell her how much I miss Dada, sure that she veils the same misery as carefully as I do. His name is now unspoken, too painful to utter. I wish she'd tell me.

The Absence of Stars

The bobbing of distant lights prompts fragile murmurings from the wandering crowd – too hushed to be interpreted as excitement, more cautious, guarded hopefulness. Hope can be dangerous in this place.

Sometimes the cars come, their inhabitants with clean, worried faces and laced-up shoes. They rarely ask us our names. They speak of 'the displaced' and communicate hurriedly about water and meagre portions of food, just enough for most to ward off starvation for a few more days. Some have energy to scramble and jostle; others sit hopelessly, forlornly and wait. Mama worries about BeBe. There's a fine line between patient and listless, she says. I know she hopes the people will notice him, his striking chestnut eyes. But to them, he's just the same as us, as all the others. He'll be counted, of course, he'll be one of the numbers on a report in an office somewhere. Perhaps they'll see a photograph of his small face in my Mama's frail arms, against her sunken chest. They'll portray sympathy. They'll tell the world what they're doing to help us while their bellies are full of fine food and their carefree children splash merrily in swimming pools.

We went to a swimming pool once, in the good days, before BeBe came and the lake disappeared. Dada could lift me back then. His strong arms would hurl me in the air and wait for me to padoosh into the pool. Water and laughter, those happy companions.

Dada and Mama would often talk about the world changing, with worried, frowning faces. Dada would urge Mama to leave. Where? How? There were no answers, and so we stayed. And as we stayed, waiting for some miracle, the waters slowly, surely, withdrew to an unknown place and took all life with them.

It Means the World to Us

Mama sleeps restlessly. "We'll be fine, Effy, don't you worry child," she murmurs. BeBe stirs. I touch his warm cheek. His face is so smooth, its gentle curves so beautiful. He has long eyelashes like Mama, full lips like Dada. Even in this deserted wilderness we have our desperate, ferocious love for each other – our greatest, most cherished gift also our heaviest burden. I cuddle into Mama, enjoying the closeness, missing her cushiony comfort of old. She often hums gently. I don't know if she's awake or asleep. Her honeyed, subdued melodies bring comfort to all of us, not just BeBe. She sleeps with her bent knuckle in his mouth, reassurance for both of them alike.

"Sleep, child," Mama urges, in her calm, comforting voice, careful not to wake BeBe. I don't think BeBe will wake. He sleeps a lot now. When he was first born his cries could wake the whole town. His ham-hock legs would pound the air like lively little pistons. Dada would laugh his deep laugh and scoop him up, high in the air, delaying his feed for a few more minutes so that Mama could get some sleep.

"You're a greedy one!" he'd say proudly. BeBe would coo and dribble before recommencing his angry, hungry wails.

I stifle sobs as I contemplate life without them, my greatest fear. Mama would never give up on us, she tells me often. We saw a mother thrusting her baby at the clean people in cars once. "Take her! Please take her!" the lady cried desperately. Mama watched quietly and steadily, drawing BeBe closer to her chest, signalling silently for me to walk beside her, slightly quickening her pace. Her big, serious eyes watching cautiously. I hadn't thought that pity was possible while in suffering.

Dada tried hard not to give up. He was unlucky, Mama said. The simple wooden cross in the dusty ground haunts me still.

The Absence of Stars

I clench my eyes shut and push the image as far into the recesses of my mind as I possibly can, pleading with someone, anyone, to make this endless ache stop.

How could our land turn on us like this? We nurtured it, worked with it, toiled together – relied on each other. Didn't we? This brutal savagery after so many years of gentle, careful cultivation. Mama says it's not our fault, but that it's not the fault of the land either. Some say it's God. Others say Man. Whoever it is, this punishment is surely excessive. Did we deserve it?

As dawn breaks, we wearily ready ourselves for a day that is both new and same. Mama glances around her, silently surveying the size of the wandering crowd, taking in the numbers who have not risen from their slumber. "We must never give up, Effy," Mama urges.

And so it goes on, Mama, BeBe and me, numbers in a crowd, lost in a land that withered and burned long ago. We watch for the lights, for the flickers of hope, for the calls of sustenance for the displaced. I selfishly rejoice that our footsteps continue, no matter their pain, and contemplate the vast expanse of the smoke-filled sky, a sky that, like my Mama's love, has no beginning or end, that holds so much shrouded beauty, its stars cloaked into smoky submission by the belligerent neglect of ignorant beings far removed from the beauty of the land that they claim to govern.

"We'll see the stars again, Mama. I know it."

THE MONSTER WHO MOVED TO ECOTOWN

Eleanor Cullen

Children's literature category for 19–24 years

Everyone in Ecotown wanted to help the planet thrive.
By keeping their carbon footprint at a healthy level five.

Because in Ecotown's town square, there was a statue standing tall.
It showed the town's energy use, and the carbon level reached by them all.
The lower the level was, the more the Earth was protected.
So level five meant all was well, whereas 50 would make it neglected!

But one day a monster bought a house in Ecotown, you see.
And on the day he did, the statue's level reached 33!
Everyone in Ecotown was shocked and a little mad.
Who was undoing their work? And making their carbon level bad?

The mayor, called Mr Marvellous, managed to calm his people down.
He said "Let me handle this!" and marched to the house with a frown.
With a rap-tap-tap he knocked on the door, though he sounded quieter than a mouse.
Because crashes, bangs and pops were heard, all coming from inside the house!

The Monster Who Moved to Ecotown

"You have to change whatever you're doing," shouted the mayor to the monster inside.
"You're hurting the world and that's very bad, but I can help you stop!" he cried.
The front door opened with a creak and a furry head popped out.
It had six horns and big black spots, and a hairy, scary snout.

"What do you mean?" asked the monster, his voice sad and slow.
"I'm living how I've always lived, but I don't want to hurt the world I know."
His eyes were deep and sorrowful, and he shuffled out of the door.
The mayor then saw the cause of the noise: machines covering the floor!

There were tumble dryers all tumbling, and taps left drip-drip-dripping.
So, he ran inside the house and did some quick switch-flipping.
Then he came back out, and held the monster's furry hand.
"Come look around the town," he said, "and learn how to care for our land."

The monster followed the mayor, bewildered but happy to change.
And they arrived at their first stop, a house the monster thought was strange.
It belonged to Windy Wendy, and it sat atop a hill.
It had wind turbines all around. "They make electricity," said the mayor. "It's brill!"

It Means the World to Us

Then he pointed to Wendy's washing lines, and the clothes that
   flapped in the breeze.
"And, instead of using dryers, she dries her washing using these!"

So that night, the monster went home, and swapped his dryers
   for turbines.
 Then he took some string and some pegs, and made some
   makeshift washing lines!
The next morning in Ecotown, the carbon footprint level shrank.
It was now at level 20, a still undesirable rank.

The mayor saw the monster again, with his head hung in dismay.
"I'm afraid you have more work to do," he said, leading him away.
They found Watery Will, who lived beside a stream.
"He gets energy from water," said the mayor. "It's his own planet-
   saving scheme."

"And he takes showers instead of baths, and waters his plants using
   saved rain!
If you want to stop wasting water, you should do that again and
   again."

So that night, the monster went home, and left watering cans in
   his yard.
He turned the tap off to brush his teeth, and found saving water
   wasn't hard.

The next morning in Ecotown, the carbon level fell again.
Though not at five, it had improved, for it was now at level 10.

The Monster Who Moved to Ecotown

The mayor saw the monster again, and heard his house had quietened down.
"I know where we should go today," he said, and they walked through Ecotown.
They stopped by the house of Sunny Sam, which had solar panels catching light.
"She gets power from the sun," said the mayor. "And keeps the spare to use in the night."

"And she uses the sun in other ways," he said, pointing towards some bees.
"To grow flowers so insects pollinate, and so we can breathe with ease!"

So that night, the monster went home, and planted seeds to grow flowers and trees.
Then he rang an energy company, and said "I'd like some solar panels, please!"

The next morning in Ecotown, the carbon level dropped even more.
It wasn't quite at level five, but that's because it was level four!
The mayor saw the monster again, a huge smile lighting up his face.
"I've one more journey for you," he said, then took him to the statue's place.

The people of Ecotown cheered, when they saw the monster approach.
"There's our hero!" they shouted out. "Our planet-saving coach!"
"How did you do it?" one person asked, the monster saw it was Sunny Sam.
He looked at the mayor, who nodded, then he said, "Well, madame.

It Means the World to Us

You use the sun to be responsible," he said, with a large beam.
Then he turned to Watery Will. "And you use water, like your stream!"
He looked for Windy Wendy, who was amongst the townspeople too.
"And Wendy uses wind power, another responsible thing to do."

"What I did that worked so well was use all three together.
I used the sun, the wind and water, to help Earth, whatever the weather!"
He then explained to Ecotown everything he'd learnt from the mayor.
How planting flowers, taking showers, and wind turbines were good for the air.

So that night all the townspeople did the same as the monster had done.
And the very next day, they all shouted "yay!", 'cause their carbon footprint reached level one.

WILLOW

Laura Hall

Children's literature category for 25+ years

Once, there was a girl who grew up in a forest.

She didn't have a mum or dad, or brothers and sisters. She didn't have an aunt or an uncle, or a granny or a grandad. All she knew was the forest, its trees, and its creatures. They were her home and her family.

Her name was Willow.

Willow was wild, and she didn't care who knew it.

When the wind blew, she danced. When the sun shone, she jumped off the cliff into the river to make the biggest splash she could. When it was quiet, she whooped into the canyon as loudly as she could to hear the words 'Willow, Willow, Willow' come echoing back.

When she felt mischievous, she chased the squirrels to the highest branches of the tallest trees and tickled the trout in the river until they cried for mercy. She hid in the bushes and jumped out at the deer as they walked past, sending them hopping and jumping high in the air.

The elder animals, the old stag and the wise raven said she should be quieter and learn to listen more. They said she should be a little bit less like herself, and a little bit more like the fawn, who sat peacefully by herself most afternoons, or the owl, who slept in the day and was almost as silent in the night when it hunted in the trees.

But Willow was wild, and she didn't care who knew it. She rode the black ponies in the pouring rain, and stamped her feet

It Means the World to Us

when she was hungry, catching the ripe apples in her hands as they fell from the trees.

One day, a strange noise filled the air.

Willow woke up with a start. The noise was loud and getting louder. It was also getting closer.

The noise started out with a sound like a very loud and raspy bird with a terrible cough and sore throat. And it ended with a crash and splintering sounds so loud that the whole forest floor was shaking. Willow, who wasn't afraid of anything, had a funny feeling in her tummy.

There, in a clearing in the forest, stood five men.

They had three chainsaws between them, and a big mechanical digger, and a clipboard. They wore helmets as yellow as a blackbird's beak. And all around them, the ancient oak trees had been felled.

At the sight of her beloved home being destroyed, Willow felt a new kind of wildness pounding in her ears. Her toes tingled and her fingers fidgeted with a strange kind of new energy. All her wild feelings came together – her wild love of the woods, a wild energy and a wild anger that anyone could come and take away something that wasn't theirs to take.

Willow opened her mouth and screamed so loudly that lightning ran jagged across the sky.

She clapped her hands and stamped her feet and terrible earthquakes zigzagged across the ground.

She clenched her hands into fists and cried hot tears of rage, and purple clouds gathered overhead, thunder boomed and torrents of rain fell to the earth.

The men looked up in terror. As they ran away, lightning scorched the ground near the soles of their boots.

Willow

Exhausted, Willow fell into a deep sleep in a dark place and slept for what seemed like forever.

She slept for so long that the animals of the forest thought she might have run away.

It was very quiet without her.

Old stag and wise raven thought about how they had asked Willow to be quieter and to be more like the fawn and the owl, and how they had been wrong.

Without Willow's wild anger, there would have been nobody to chase away the men.

Without Willow's fearless behaviour, there would have been nobody to protect the forest.

Maybe being wild and noisy and not very good at sitting still wasn't such a bad thing after all, they thought. Maybe her wild spirit was exactly what the forest needed to protect it and keep it strong.

When Willow finally woke up, she found her forest full of gentle birdsong and sunshine. The trees that had fallen were now overgrown with mushrooms and toadstools. Wildflowers and saplings grew in the sunny spots they had left.

As she looked around in quiet amazement at the beautiful forest, a wild and carefree song started to bubble up in her chest. She threw her head back and sang as loudly as she could, so that every inch of the forest would know she was alive, and back to protect it with everything she had.

Far away in the distance, old stag and wise raven heard her voice and decided to sing along too.

MARSHA'S PLAN TO SAVE THE SEA

Jenna Thirtle

Children's literature category for 19–24 years

Marsha sat in awe as her Grandpa told her stories of the sea. When he was much younger, he used to take his little boat out on the big blue sea and catch fish for her dad and uncle.

But Marsha didn't believe him. The only boats Marsha had seen in the sea were enormous noisy ones.

"And one day a dolphin jumped right over my head!" Grandpa told her.

Marsha had never seen a dolphin before!

"Grandpa, where have all the dolphins gone?" Marsha asked.

"The big, noisy boats have scared them away! They have also taken all their food!" Grandpa looked sad.

"There used to be whales, and all sorts of fish here, they have all gone now though."

Marsha was sad, she wanted to see dolphins and whales!

"Don't worry Grandpa I will get the fish back!" Marsha said.

When Marsha went home she told her mum about her plan to save the sea.

The next day in school Marsha told all her friends about her plan.

"My Grandpa said there used to be whales!" she said excitedly to her friends.

"WOW," they were all shocked!

"Well, my Grandma said there were animals with eight wiggly legs that used to live in the sea!" Koen told the group.

Marsha's Plan to Save the Sea

"Wow! I wonder what other animals used to live in the sea!" Marsha replied.

They all sat and imagined how amazing it would be to save the sea. They needed a plan.

Marsha took out her little piece of paper and showed the group.

"We need to write a plan. My Grandpa said the noisy ships are to blame!"

Koen replied, "My Grandpa said there is too much rubbish in the sea and the animals don't like it."

"My uncle told me the water is too hot, it is like they are having a really hot bath!" Kirra told the group.

"I don't like baths," said Koen.

How do we stop these things?" asked Marsha.

"Maybe we tell the big ships they can only use small boats, like your Grandpa Marsh," said Koen.

"Good idea," replied Marsha.

"And maybe we can add some cold water to the sea! That will make it colder for the fish!" said Kirra.

Everyone nodded. "Good idea Kirra."

"Then we collect all the rubbish in the sea," Marsha said.

"YEY," everyone cheered!

Plan to save the sea
1. Tell the people in the big boats they can only use little boats.
2. Add cold water to the sea to make it colder.
3. Ask Grandpa if we can borrow his boat to collect all the rubbish in the sea.

Everyone was very happy with the plan.

When Marsha got home, she showed her mum.

It Means the World to Us

"Marsha, you cannot do these things. You are too little," her mum said.

Marsha was sad. She really wanted to save the sea.

A few days later her Grandpa came for tea.

"Have you got a plan to save the sea Marsha?" her Grandpa asked.

"Yes, but mum said I am too little," Marsha replied sadly.

Grandpa shook his head. "Do not be silly. Anyone can help save the sea."

Marsha smiled, and she ran to get the plan she and her friends at school made.

Grandpa looked closely at the plan. He chuckled. "This is an excellent plan, Marsha. I am proud of you."

Marsha smiled her biggest smile. "When can we start Grandpa?"

"Well can I change one or two things?" Grandpa asked.

"Hmmm, okay," said Marsha. She ran to get a new piece of paper and a pen.

Plan to save the sea
1. Start a petition to stop so many big boats in one area.
2. Ask mum to buy from local fishers and other local shops.
3. Recycle as much as possible.
4. Use less single-use plastics.
5. Pick up rubbish on the beach.

Grandpa showed Marsha the new list. "What do you think?" he asked.

"I do not understand how these things will help, Grandpa," Marsha replied.

"OK, I will explain them to you."

"To stop the big ships, we need to talk to the people in charge.

Marsha's Plan to Save the Sea

They set the limit on the boats in the area. The more people who help us the better! That is a petition, people who agree sign their name."

"Oh, OK! Yes, I like that idea," Marsha said.

"Good! Okay, number two. The food in big supermarkets sometimes has to travel a long way to get there. This can cause a lot of pollution and make the sea hot. If we buy from local shops, the food does not travel far. This does not create as much pollution, stopping the sea from getting hot. I do not think we have enough cold water to make the water colder," Grandpa explained.

"You are right we do not have enough cold water. You are very clever Grandpa!" Marsha liked idea number two.

"Thank you," Grandpa smiled at her. "Now, numbers three and four. If we recycle the rubbish will not end up in the ocean, it will get disposed of properly. And if we use less single-use plastics, it means fewer things are being put in the rubbish that might end up in the ocean."

"That will stop the dolphins from being sad!" said Marsha.

"Yes exactly," Grandpa replied.

"Finally, number five. We can go and collect all the bits of rubbish on the beach. This will stop it from being caught by the waves and taken off to sea."

Marsha thought about the new plan. She wanted to talk to her friends first and see if they agreed.

"Thank you, Grandpa. I will take this new list to school and ask my friends."

Grandpa smiled, "Of course! This is your plan to save the sea. Let me know what they say."

The next day Marsha showed everyone the new plan.

It Means the World to Us

"I am sorry Kirra, Grandpa said we did not have enough cold water," said Marsha.

"It's OK. I like this plan better," Kirra replied with a smile.

Everyone really liked Grandpa's new plan. They all agreed that they would go to the beach and collect all the rubbish they could find at the weekend.

Their teacher heard them talking about their plan. She thought it was a fantastic idea. She went straight to the headteacher to tell her all about it.

That weekend, Marsha, her Grandpa, and her friends went to the beach to collect the rubbish.

When they got to the beach, they were surprised at what they saw. The whole school was there picking up rubbish!

The school headteacher had sent a message to all the parents at the school telling them about Marsha's plan and asked for some help.

Everyone thought Marsha's plan was fantastic; they all wanted the fish, dolphins, whales, and other sea creatures to come back and be happy in the sea!

PALE BLUE DOT

Philip Williams

Poetry category for 25+ years

> *I would send the complete works of Johann Sebastian Bach into outer space on the Voyager spacecraft. But that would be boasting.*
> Lewis Thomas, 1977.

For all we know they might prefer White Noise,
assuming they have stylus, turntable
and deck to spin Earth's golden phonograph.
Or choose Mozart, Stravinsky, Beethoven
from the pressed disc of our selected hits.
Perhaps the pygmy girls' initiation song
might appeal to them, Senegalese
percussion, Georgian choir, Chuck Berry,
blues, raga, bagpipes from Azerbaijan.

Might they receive our coded boast as threat,
a declaration of war, or raw rasp
of shapeless sound? Perhaps they purr
and pulse soundwaves among themselves,
or are themselves pure sound, humming
soft vibrations across the solar void like whales.
Or else communicate by touch, antennae,
telepathy, absorb thought through porous skins,
sift sense and sequences through membranes.

It Means the World to Us

Colour may convey their currency, a shaded commerce
lit by twin suns for compound eyes. Might they inhabit
the gaps between keys on well-tempered boards,
know no chromatic scales but only silence?
Our iconography may alarm them. Images of crowded
cities, traffic, our reproductive system, hunting.
If they were bent on interstellar war, then Bach
may soothe them, harmonise our harsh fuzz
and fuse it into a fugue of peace.

Then, they may seek us, thrust through deep space
to the sound of claviers to where our blue orb
spins and beckons bright.

Will they arrive too late, trace scant echoes,
our diminuendo, our falling cadence only,
from the dark side of the moon?

DUIR

Helen Kay

Poetry category for 25+ years

The news of an oak branch, ripped by hungry
gales and the trunk that grows sealed lips.

A drama of wasp's eggs hatching in bark,
of larva that builds its own gall wombhouse.

A saga of knots that warp the tree's rings,
of a gnarled burl, swollen round the trunk.

A psalm of soil eroded, roots exposed,
scarfed by mosses and liverworts.

A tale of when the horsefly bit me,
and crushed oak leaves soothed the sores.

A prayer of how the druid, dryad tree
lets my dried out head be moist again.

INTERVIEW

Cathy Bryant

Short story category for 25+ years

"Hello. My name is Hari 175," I said. "I'd like to apply for death, please."

She pressed buttons.

"You've filled in the forms, I see. That's great, Hari, but there is an interview too."

"I know. I'm prepared."

I tried to sound confident and responsible, though I felt anything but.

"You've got Jack 84," said the woman at the desk, and gave me a sympathetic look. She was nice.

I had no idea who Jack 84 might be; I'd just turned up when the computer had told me I should, only to find this archaic world of desk, receptionist and waiting room. Bureaucracy is always light years behind culture.

I sat and waited, humming tunelessly to myself. An annoying habit, but I wasn't used to downtime like this. Of course I took the requisite periods of sleep, meditation, and free-talking with my wife, like any good citizen.

Lin. I could call her.

"Lin 207," I said to the phone, and her face appeared, lined with worry.

"Darling," I said, "I'm waiting for my interview."

"If you're successful, then I'll never see you again," she whispered. "I can't bear it. I love you so much, Hari."

Interview

"And I you. Oh, Lin, the choices we have to make! I know it's our own fault, but –"

"No it isn't!" she cried. "It was our stupid ancestors. How could they? I just don't understand how they could do this to us."

"No one does. Oh –" – a light had appeared at the desk, and the receptionist had raised her eyebrows to alert me. "I have to go. Goodbye, darling."

"Goodbye, my love."

I closed the phone on my life.

"Jack 84 will see you now," said the receptionist, sounding like something from an old movie. "The door with the green handle."

I thanked her and went 'to my doom' as I thought of it, rather theatrically.

Jack 84 was a short woman with a no-nonsense expression and cropped white hair. Like most of us, she probably used her hair to stuff mattresses, pillows and cushions.

"Sit down, Hari," she said. "I'm Jack."

Her smile was swift, professional and anything but reassuring.

"Pleased to meet you," I said, and shook her hand. I tried to mirror her smile, but felt as if I were made of very thin glass that could shatter at any moment, and that she could see this.

"I've been reviewing your application," she said. "You give your reason for death as birth. You wish to be replaced by a child. Is that correct?"

"Yes. My child with my wife. I have sperm waiting ready at the bank, and my wife is at optimal fertility, we think."

"You are a doctor. Is that right?"

Why did she ask when the answer was no doubt on a screen in front of her?

"Part time. I also do recycling, as well as helping at harvest time, of course."

It Means the World to Us

"A useful mix."

"I hope so."

There was a pause while Jack frowned, staring at the screen that I couldn't see.

"Medical training is lengthy and expensive. You are very useful to society, and could continue to be so for two or three more decades."

"I know – but I've worked for 22 years since I qualified. My wife is a teacher, and very healthy. Our child is almost certain to be clever and useful. As I said, my wife is at optimal fertility –"

"That isn't relevant," said Jack, but she spoke softly, and seemed sympathetic for the first time.

"It should be! I am willing to sacrifice my life in order to father a child. Now is the best possible time. Isn't it as simple as that?"

"Perhaps it should be, but it isn't."

As you know, natural resources are so limited now that society has to be run as efficiently as possible to ensure our survival. Personal desires come second to that. The population needs to be reduced, not expanded, and the least harsh way to do that is to limit childbirth. Yes, in some circumstances one can give one's life in order to make way for a child. Many of the elderly have done so. They are heroes. But if we are to feed, shelter and have enough air for the remainder of the populace, then we must keep our most efficient workers."

My anger and frustration threatened to burst out of me.

"So because I've worked hard and been useful, I can't have a child?"

"If you hadn't, then you wouldn't have stood a chance," said Jack firmly. "Only the healthy and efficient are allowed to breed – sometimes."

Interview

A tear fought its way out of my eyes and tried to escape down my cheek.

"When I was a boy, I had a friend. She was in a wheelchair and couldn't move her limbs. She had a job, but also needed care. She wasn't allowed 'to breed' as you put it, either."

Jack said nothing, but let me pour it out.

"She – her name was Petra – sang with the sweetest voice you ever heard. She could have sung to her children. I don't know where she is now or what happened to her ... I've been so busy ... "

I passed my hand over my face, and my desperation threw out one more question.

"What price survival? What have we given up?"

"If we relax the rules, then we all starve or asphyxiate," said Jack. "The air factories, soy farms and water reclaimers can only do so much. But please don't despair."

I looked at her, my eyes dull.

"If we are careful now and work hard, then in the future people may all have a child, and sing to them. That's what we work towards – as much freedom as is compatible with responsible use of resources, until we have repaired the devastating damage our forebears did to the planet.

"As for your application – I've done everything I can. Our reports on you indicate that your conduct is excellent. You are prudent and thrifty – you darn and mend clothes that are old and well-used, I can see, even though you could apply for newer ones. And I note that your phone is shared between 20 people, and charges by winding.

You are, in fact, a model citizen, as is your wife. We just need a little longer from you. Come back in five years, Hari, and the requirements will all be fulfilled."

"It might be too late to have a child by then."

It Means the World to Us

"It's never certain anyway. It never was, even when fertility treatments were legal. You just have to hope."

She rose, indicating that the interview was over.

"In the meantime, Hari, enjoy your life, and don't forget to sing."

"I have a terrible voice. Thanks anyway," I said, shook her hand, and left. Dazed, I strode past the kind receptionist, who called out a goodbye, and I began the long walk home.

I couldn't face phoning Lin. It would be a waste of resources, as I'd see her soon anyway.

Suicide was out of the question. There was no more certain way to exclude yourself (and sometimes your whole family) from having a child. But I felt the idea of it come close, brushing me with its cold wing.

One thing that helped me was the kindness of the people I met on the walk home. It is customary now to smile at strangers, and to ask if they need anything. I asked for nothing except a handshake or a hug, though any of them would have listened to my story, had I needed emotional support. In that way we are richer than the people of the past, if history is to be believed. I cannot believe it, though. Surely people were never in fear of each other, and trying to take each other's possessions all the time. How could anyone achieve happiness that way? The idea is cynical and silly, I think.

So my spirits lifted a little as I walked along. Life is not as bad as I feel it is, sometimes. And I did sing, a terrific, terrible, winding tune that soon tied me up in knots – of laughter, even.

When I opened the door of our apartment (two rooms! Kitchen and living/sleeping room. The bathroom was, naturally, shared and the water rationed), Lin gave a cry like a seabird, and flew into my arms.

Interview

"They said to come back in five years."

We wept together, and then Lin's amazing optimism kicked in.

"I'm so glad to have you, even if we can't have a child yet, or at all," she whispered, and smiled at me. She cradled my head and sang an old love song to me, and I managed to smile too, feeling the preciousness of life, and the fragments of joy that can turn up even on the grimmest days. In so many ways, so very many ways – we are lucky.

SALVAGED

Eve Naden

Short story category for 19–24 years

Mum stares at me through bottle-caps. One eye of sparkling water, the other Diet Coke. She doesn't blink.

We sit on the veranda, watching as they fell the trees. They fall like dominoes, one by one by one. Making way for the Weston Woods – that's what it says on the leaflets. Three hundred new homes. Fresh materials, suitable housing. Brand-spanking-new prices – buy one get one free! Affordable homes for all, it says; four-bedroom bungalows for only £300,000!

I lean into Mum. Her skin twists, knotting at the elbows. Her cardboard shoes tap on the wood panelling. Nana and Grandad built this place. Left it to Mum, then to me. I can't inherit till I'm 29, so Mum keeps me company.

"Would you like some tea?" I ask. I'm surprised when she nods. Her head is round and large, the flesh red and puckered. She prefers the tea she makes herself. Calls mine 'gnat's wee'.

I place bricks on her hands and feet to keep her there. Then I head into the house. Plaster stripped down to chipboard mingles with the dwindling sunlight. We're redecorating. Mum wants an oceanic theme, but I'd like something a little brighter. We mix flowers in bottles to make the paints. I'll get started on the kitchen tomorrow.

I grab the kettle and head down the hall, out the front door. The driveway is peppered with dandelions, creeping buttercups and thyme.

Salvaged

Mum's car sits in the driveway, barely used. It isn't charging, and I can see Mr and Mrs Andrews, our neighbours to the left, shaking their heads.

I couldn't afford to run it if I tried. Why do they think I'm carrying the kettle to the river?

It's a mile away and I walk with the wind, listening to its rhythm. The kettle grows sullen in my hands, waiting. A mile isn't too far – it's what we used to run in school. It's better for me. To get out of the house and away from her.

Mum needs her space.

The river bleeds behind the village hall. A bridge stretches across it, from where we used to play pooh-sticks. Mum would always win.

Kneeling, I fill the kettle to the top. Carry it with both hands this time, back to the cul-de-sac.

I'm almost there when someone catches my arm and pulls me towards them. I almost drop the kettle.

"What are you doing?" asks my uncle. Adam Forbes is tall, with strips of obsidian for eyebrows. Fingers stained with nicotine, but his face is bright. My cousin is behind him. Cousin Iris, the eldest. Only three years younger than me. All blonde-hair, miniskirts, and sandals – like some mosquito from one of those magazines.

But the girl with her hand around my wrist is Eve. She lives four streets away, practically in the next village.

"What's going on?" I ask. "Ganging up on us now, are you?" Adam has never missed a chance to humiliate his sister, my mother. With a single look, he can wrinkle her skin and pop her teeth like balloons. Ever since Mum bought the car – no, before that. When we started shopping at the farm and I wore dead Aunt Jane's dungarees to school, even though they smelt

It Means the World to Us

like weed. But Adam … Just because we stopped going to the supermarket (he only calls it 'his supermarket' because he works there. He isn't even the manager) we are strangers.

"We just want to talk," is what he says now. I laugh, wrenching myself from Eve's grip.

"You can't just ignore this," says Iris. She's 20 now. How old am I, then?

"Look. I need to get back. Mum's waiting." She'll float away if I don't return soon. She lives from moment to moment, you know. Once that moment passes, she'll want coffee, not tea. And we have no coffee.

Eve follows, offering to carry the kettle. I hug it closer to my chest.

"Slow down, will you? We need to talk." Iris. She sounds just like her father.

When we reach the drive, I hear their footsteps fade. I look back and they're staring.

"We're redecorating," I snap. Grandad wouldn't want us to, but Nana would, and I must honour each of them somehow. Mum says compromise is the way forward, so we're redecorating half the house and keeping the other half frozen in mothballs – just how Grandad would have liked it.

"Anna." My uncle follows me down the drive. "Anna, wait."

"What happened to the car?" asks Iris. I shrug.

"I can't drive. What use is it to me?"

"You passed your test," Eve points out. "Why won't you drive?"

I glare. This is why we stopped being friends in the first place. Too curious (which I believe is the kindest word for nosy) for her own good.

My shoulders sag. Mum wouldn't want me to ignore our guests.

"Would you like to come in?" I ask. "I'll put the kettle on."

Salvaged

The three of them exchange glances, but it's Eve, to my surprise, who agrees first. The others follow, though my uncle spends a good minute or two staring at the car. Its cracked windscreen and the scratches down one side. I don't see why he's concerned. I'm not going to be driving it around if that's what he's worried about. His little niece, parading around in that monstrosity – what on earth would people think?

"Come on through. To the veranda," I add. They follow, almost in single file. Eve actually smiles as she spots the compost toilet (home-made) and the recycled wallpaper (tissues and clothes I'm now too thin to fit). Uncle Adam is not smiling. He's pale and practically green.

"She's through here. Mum, we have company! No, of course I haven't forgotten your tea. I'll make it now." I head outside and place the kettle in the fire pit I built. There's wire mesh over it, taken from Mum's old bike. She doesn't cycle anymore. I place the kettle on the mesh and sit down to light the fire. All I can do is hope a wind doesn't pick up.

Uncle Adam is walking towards the bench, where Mum is sat, pinned by bricks. Her transparent arms glow in the sun and, from this angle, she's smiling. I close my eyes and picture her pencil-like lips expanding and contracting as she says,

"Oh, Ad. I'm so happy to see you. I'm not sure why, but I am."

Instead, all I get is,

"Anna, sweetheart. What have you done?" I flinch. It's the first time anyone's called me that since …

I ignore it and hunker over the yet-to-exist flames. I'll get the hang of this. Like Mum says: it's all about persistence.

"Anna, stop it." Arms wrap around my waist. Eve is pulling me back, away from the fire and the kettle.

"I need to get Mum a cup of tea. Haven't you been listening?"

It Means the World to Us

I say. But then I see cousin Iris, who's sat next to Mum, crying. Her blonde hair is matted, and I realise she's wearing rubber bands instead of those plastic bracelets. Eve is wearing those tights I bought her – made from fishing twine. And Adam is sitting on the wall, staring at his tyre-coloured shoes.

"We should have come sooner," he whispers.

Perhaps they've noticed. Noticed that my mother is two cardboard boxes, 10 plastic bags filled with water and soil, a balloon for a head, broken pencils for lips and those bottle-caps, blinking in earnest.

"She worked 18-hour days." The words come before I can stop them. "She threw her back out. And all to afford that stupid car? All to shop at the overpriced farm?" I think of the day I found her, cold and grey. A heart attack at 55, after 20 years in that hospital. That ultimatum. The day she finally switched out the petrol car for the one sat in our drive. She died two days later.

I slump to the floor.

Eve leaves me there, but my uncle sits next to me.

"You don't have to do this alone," he says. He digs in his pocket and takes out a leaflet. It's for the supermarket. An advertisement about lowering prices on organic produce. "I'm manager now. I have a bit of leeway. You're not alone, kiddo."

I lean into his shoulder, watching my cousin lift the bricks from Mum's hands and feet.

AWARENESS

Beth Westbrook

Scriptwriting category for 19–24 years

CAST

AURORA, 17
EMMA, 42
AVA, 18
COMMENTER, All ages, A chorus of actors, An encapsulation of the online world.

The following roles can be played by separate actors or multi-roled:

DAD
MICHAEL
UNIVERSITY ADMISSION TEAM (UAT)
PRODUCER
PRESENTER

Aurora and Ava should be played by autistic/neurodivergent, female identifying actors. These are the only characters specifically written to be disabled, but feel free to cast more disabled actors.

The following is an extract from the full script submitted to the competition.

ACT 1
1.
Filtered World/Unfiltered World.

AURORA breathes in,
One. Two. Three. Four.
Holds her breath.

One. Two. Three. Four.
And breathes out.
One. Two. Three. Four.
A phone unlocks.

AURORA watches a video. We hear a young girl crying.
Knock, Knock.

EMMA enters.
We find ourselves in Aurora's bedroom. It's only lit by a bedside lamp.

EMMA: Ironed your skirt for tomorrow.

AURORA: Thanks.

EMMA: Get off your phone or you won't sleep.

AURORA: I will. I'm just finding a sleep meditation. Think I've gone through them all.

EMMA: Alright. Ni-Night.

AURORA: Night.

EMMA closes the door shut behind her.

AURORA debates whether to put her phone down and go to sleep. She doesn't put her phone down.
Phone unlocks again.

COMMENTER: Bless her

2.
Unfiltered World.

Alarm goes off.
Aurora's bedroom is now fully lit.

Awareness

We can see the bedroom is immaculately organised. There's a school timetable, and a daily timetable up on the wall.

EMMA is fully dressed, and is helping AURORA pack her school bag.

AURORA is putting her make-up on. It clatters on the table.

AURORA: S***!

EMMA: Aurora!

AURORA: I've got make-up on my top!

EMMA: Don't worry, there's another top which will go.

AURORA: The one with lace at the top? No, it won't go!

AURORA starts to take her top off.

EMMA: I meant the cream one with the cuff things.

AURORA: Oh yeah.

AURORA opens the wardrobe and puts on a new shirt.

EMMA: Are we on Week A or Week B?

AURORA: I don't know 'cause we don't know if we start from Week A after half term again, or carry on to Week B.

EMMA: What if you take in all your books to school today?

AURORA: College. And no. My bag'll be heavy and if I bring everything in I'll focus on everything badly instead of properly focusing on one thing good.

EMMA: OK so you definitely have Psychology today.

AURORA: What? I never have Psychology on a Monday.

EMMA: It says you always have Psychology on a Monday.

It Means the World to Us

AURORA'S chest tightens. Her breath hitches. She starts to stim slightly, her bracelet jingles.

AURORA: I didn't finish my practice paper.

EMMA: You were supposed to time yourself doing it.

AURORA: Everyone said they weren't going to time themselves so if I timed myself I'd do awful and be put at the bottom of the class and Michael hates me anyway and he'd try and make me drop it again.

EMMA: You have a free period before lunch, you can finish it then.

EMMA puts the folders in AURORA'S bag, and zips it shut.
   What are you doing for lunch today?

AURORA: I think we're going to Domino's as a first-day back treat.

EMMA: Won't that give you a headache? The MSG always gives you a headache.

AURORA: It won't.

EMMA: Fine. Just be careful because you're already stressed.

AURORA: No I'm not.
Doorbell rings.

EMMA: Ready?

AURORA: I just need to chuck some shoes on.

EMMA: You should do some breathing exercises.

AURORA: I can do them in the car!

EMMA: They won't work in the car – you should do them now before it gets too much.

Awareness

AURORA: Dad can do them with me.

EMMA: No! Do them with me.

AURORA: NO! I DON'T HAVE TIME!
Sorry.
Fine.

EMMA: Breathe in.

EMMA counts on her fingers as the pair breathe in
> One. Two. Three. Four.
> Hold.

EMMA makes a signal to hold the breath –
One. Two. Three. Four.
Breathe out.
And then a signal to breathe out –
One. Two. Three. Four.
Once more.
In.
Breathe in –
> One. Two. Three. Four.
> Hold.
Hold –
> One. Two.

The doorbell rings again aggressively.

AURORA'S breathing becomes more rapid and she starts to have a panic attack.

EMMA: Take your time. He'll wait. Breathe in
One. Two. Three. Four.
Hold.
Hold –

It Means the World to Us

It's not working too well, Aurora's breath catches –
One. Two. Three. Four.
Out.
Breathe out –
One. Two. Three. Four.

AURORA'S breaths are shaky.
    OK. Don't panic.

AURORA starts to panic more.

Aurora, name five things you can see.

AURORA: You. My school bag. The dirty shirt. My make-up. My table.

EMMA: Good. Now four things you can touch.

AURORA: My skirt. My hair. The wall. My shoes.

EMMA: Good. Three things you can hear.

AURORA: You. Dad.

EMMA: Not including your dad.

AURORA: The radio in the kitchen. Erm.

AURORA stamps her foot.

My foot.

EMMA: Close enough. Two things you can smell.

AURORA: My perfume. Honey.

EMMA: And what can you taste?

AURORA: Toothpaste.

EMMA: Good girl.
Better?

Awareness

AURORA: Yeah.

EMMA: Do you want me to ring the school and ask if you can go in later?

AURORA shakes her head firmly.

EMMA: No. OK. What about if I ask if you can sit in Mrs Fletcher's office?

AURORA: I have a free first thing. I'll be fine. Thanks.

3.
Filtered World.

WHAT THE SCHOOL RUN IS REALLY LIKE – AUTISM – MUMMY_WITH_A_MISSION Vlog.

EMMA starts the vlog in her home studio. Copyright free music plays over the video.

EMMA: Hi mummies and little 'uns! I hope you're all OK and doing well. After all the Halloween fun, it's the end of half term which means it's back to school time which can be super stressful for children with autism, so I've shared a back-to-school routine for Aurora before, which I'll leave a link for in the bio. Although I was completely real with you guys in that vlog, you caught us on a good day. Believe me not every day is like that, so I'm going to share what our morning routine is usually like.

A phone unlocks.

COMMENTER *is online.*
Ping.

COMMENTER: You are so brave.

It Means the World to Us

AURORA'S bedroom.
This is a filtered version of Scene 2, edited by EMMA. EMMA knows this is being filmed, AURORA does not. EMMA uses jump cuts when editing the video.

AURORA is sat doing her make-up as EMMA is setting up the camera.

AURORA: Censored.

EMMA: Aurora!

AURORA: I've got make-up on my top!

EMMA: Don't worry, there's another cream top which will go with that.

COMMENTER: #AutismAwareness
Jump cut.

AURORA: No, it won't go!
Jump cut as AURORA reaches down to take her top off.

AURORA is now in the clean shirt.

EMMA: Are we on Week A or Week B?
Ping.

COMMENTER: Ah bless you

AURORA: I don't know.
Jump cut.

EMMA: What if you take in all your books to school today?
Jump cut.

AURORA: No.
Jump cut.
Close up on AURORA stimming.

Awareness

AURORA: I didn't finish my practice paper.
Ping.

COMMENTER: Xxx.
Jump cut.

AURORA: Everyone said they weren't going to time themselves so if I timed myself, I'd do awful and be put at the bottom of the class and Michael hates me anyway and he'd try and make me drop it again.
Jump cut.

EMMA: Before you go you should do some breathing exercises.
Jump cut.

AURORA: I DON'T HAVE TIME!
Ping.

COMMENTER: #AutismAwareness
Jump cut.

AURORA'S breathing becomes more rapid, and she starts to have a panic attack.
Jump cut.

EMMA: Breathe in.
The following exercise is sped up in a time lapse style. AURORA and EMMA are muted as the music plays. COMMENTER continues to comment intermittently throughout the time lapse in a chorus of pings.

COMMENTER: Follow me
Words cannot express how grateful I am for what you do.
One. Two. Three. Four.

It Means the World to Us

My 15-year-old nephew has autism and is bullied everyday but your love and support will help us get through today.
Hold.
Kids are cruel.
Please give an RT.
It's not working too well.
You make me proud to be an autistic mummy
One. Two. Three. Four.
I have a child with autism and each day is so tough
Breathe out.
Thank you!

AURORA'S breaths are shaky.
You are mum goals
I wish I was as strong as you.
One. Two. Three. Four.
You are so brave
Jump cut.
Time lapse breaks.

EMMA: Aurora, name five things you can see.
The time lapse continues from when AURORA says "You. My school bag ... "

COMMENTER: I know you probably won't see this but you have saved my life
Ah bless her
Kids need to be taught it's ok to be different
Xxx.
#AutismAwareness
The time lapse breaks after AURORA says "The radio in the kitchen."

AURORA *stamps her foot.*

Awareness

The time lapse resumes from when EMMA says "Close enough."

COMMENTER: Words cannot express how grateful I am for what you do. Ah bless her.

The time lapse stops after AURORA says "Toothpaste," as AURORA is brought out of a panic attack.

EMMA: Good girl.
   Better?

Ping.

COMMENTER: You are mum goals

AURORA: Yeah.

EMMA goes back to talking to the camera.

EMMA: Luckily, these mornings are happening less and less due to the strategies Aurora and I are using.

Ping.

COMMENTER: #AutismAwareness

EMMA: You can find the link to our strategy series in the bio. But this is still a reality for myself and the millions of mummies up and down the country.

Ping.

COMMENTER: Ah bless her.

EMMA: Please remember to like and subscribe, and I'll be popping my nose in the comments soon!

Ping.

COMMENTER: I have a child with autism and each day is so, so, so tough

EMMA: See you soon mummies and little 'uns. Mummy knows best.

4.
Unfiltered World.

DAD is driving AURORA to school. She has her headphones in.

DAD: Aurora I'm happy to continue taking you to school but you –

AURORA: College.

DAD: College, but you can't be late because then you make me late.

AURORA: I had a panic attack.

DAD: Oh.
   You alright?

AURORA: Yeah.

DAD: Right. Good. Have you ever thought of getting a bus?

AURORA: Buses give me panic attacks in the morning.

DAD: Only in the morning?

AURORA: Yeah. Weird, isn't it? Well not weird because they give me panic attacks because there's too many people. It's easier for you to give me a lift because there aren't any panic attacks.

DAD: There was today.

AURORA: But it wasn't your fault. Actually, it kind of was. But not really.

DAD: Why was it my fault?

AURORA: You knocked on the door.

DAD: *(sarcastic)* Sorry.

AURORA: And it's easier for you to give me a lift because it's on the way to work. And the car is warm.

DAD: It used to be on the way. Did you catch *Doctor Who* this weekend?

AURORA: Don't watch it anymore.

DAD: Oh right.

AURORA: Might catch up on iPlayer though. Did you like it?

DAD: Didn't watch it either. Why don't you watch it anymore, y'used to love it?

AURORA: I'm 17.

DAD: So you can watch it when you're 16, but not 17?

AURORA: I shouldn't really have been watching it over the age of 10 to be honest.

DAD: You're allowed to like what you like without worrying about what other people think.

AURORA: Oh I know, it just got s*** when they killed Amy.

5.
#ActuallyAutistic World.

Aurora's bedroom.

AURORA slumps into her bedroom, accidentally slamming the door. She flops onto the bed, the springs go. She lies there for a while, not even looking on her phone.

COMMENTER is online.
Ping.

AURORA ignores the notification.

It Means the World to Us

COMMENTER: *(Off)* #ActuallyAutistic
Ping.

COMMENTER: *(Off)* Can people stop saying people with autism? WE'RE AUTISTIC. AUTISM IS NOT A PET. #ActuallyAutistic

AURORA unlocks her phone, seeing the notification, her interest piques.
Ping.

COMMENTER: *(Off)* Autism is not a superpower. I'm proud to be autistic but can we stop pretending I'm an avenger please. #ActuallyAutistic

AURORA is online.

AURORA is typing.

AURORA: Yes.
Send message. Whoosh.
Ping.

COMMENTER: *(Off)* Yes, I'm autistic. No, it's not the worst thing to happen to me.
Typing.

AURORA: It is a bit s*** though.
Whoosh.
Ping.

COMMENTER: *(Off)* Cancer's worse though. You can't die from being autistic.
Typing.

AURORA: I know but sometimes I feel like I might die from overloads.
Whoosh.
Ping.

Awareness

COMMENTER: *(Off)* True. I just meant that I should be allowed to be my autistic self without people offering me a cure. Not a fan of drinking bleach.
Ping.

COMMENTER: *(Off)* Hands up if you're autistic but you're not like *Rain Man*. #ActuallyAutistic
Typing.

AURORA: What's *Rain Man*?
Whoosh.
Ping.

COMMENTER: *(Off)* Really? No one forced you to watch *Rain Man* as some sort of autism initiation?
Typing.

AURORA: No?
Typing.
  Wait, is he the maths guy? A teacher told me he thought I'd be the next *Rain Man* until he realised I was s*** at maths. Lol.
Whoosh.
Ping. Ping. Ping. Ping.
The pings gently continue as COMMENTER appears in AURORA'S bedroom.

AURORA is absorbed in her phone as she goes deeper into the world of the #ActuallyAutistic community. The world becomes louder, and more distinct.

COMMENTER: #ActuallyAutistic
  Hands up if you're autistic but you're not like *Rain Man*?
  Autism is not a superpower
  Functioning labels is grosser than my food touching

It Means the World to Us

Autism isn't a bad word.
#AutismAwareness
Stim to your heart's content.
I'm proud to be autistic but can we stop pretending I'm an avenger please?
Can people stop saying people with autism?
You can be autistic and s*** at maths.

Let that internalised ableism go and be your true autistic self.
Stop saying I'm like Sheldon Cooper.
It's weird for you but not for me.
Speech isn't the only form of communication.

AURORA'S hand shoots up, empowered.

AURORA: Hands up if you're autistic but you're a dumb b****!

COMMENTER: OMG. Live your dumb autistic b**** life girl!
Knock at the door.

COMMENTER *is offline.*

THE APPLE

Ben Saunders

Scriptwriting category for 25+ years

FADE IN

EXT. LOCATION #1/ – MIDDLE OF THE DAY

Summer 2123 in northern England. Two adult male figures stand on a sandstone clifftop at the Alderley Edge overlooking what used to be known as the Cheshire plain, but is now the Cheshire Fens. The area behind the cliff is forested with orderly lines of fruit trees, a pandemonium of bright green parakeets squawk loudly as they pass overhead. A huge wind turbine over a kilometre high, spins at the far end of the red cliffs, its two enormous carbon fibre blades are shaped like a silver Minoan axe, but one which is carving the air whilst being larger than the Colossus itself. In the distance the faint outline of geodesic domes are sketched out across the base of the sky, covering the skyscrapers and historic buildings of Manchester in the distance in a mesh of protective webbing.

CHARACTER #1: MERLIN

A bearded man sits atop his gleaming white 'horse' robot. He has a flowing white cloak to catch the solar radiation and power his automaton steed.

MERLIN: So … I can hardly believe what you're offering can possibly be real. I'm sure you realise the implications, the importance and just how much this could change things?

It Means the World to Us

CHARACTER #2: GIORGIO

A young-looking man with long dark hair, rugged looks which defy the convention of the day by having square jawed implants, which make him look decidedly 21st century in appearance. He does not have a robot horse and is on foot.

Giorgio momentarily ignores the question from Merlin, before touching his oversized cheeks with one hand. He tilts his head to one side but doesn't look at his companion.

GIORGIO: Oh yes, I get it alright. That's why you're here. This has taken a lot of work.

MERLIN: Good, because it's taken me an hour to ride down here across that marshland from the Manchester zone. Wasted energy electro-charging my cloak to get the thing clean of all that mud.

GIORGIO: Well at least at that speed it'd bounce off the mosquitos.

MERLIN: Yes. (sarcastically) Thank Gaia for small mercies …

GIORGIO: It's unfortunate that the mosquito is one of the few things that seem to be able to survive outdoors.

MERLIN: Not many of the things they eat can survive and breed now, though, so I don't understand what they're feeding on.

GIORGIO: Probably just the pigworms.

Even saying the word makes Giorgio shudder at the thought of them.

MERLIN: Well, enough pleasantries, let's get down to the purpose of my visit …

The Apple

The robot hisses as it slides downwards, allowing the white-robed man to stand before it shoots backwards, jumping upwards to stand to attention.

GIORGIO: Whoa! I'll never get used to those things.
Both men watch the horse without speaking and the silence is eventually broken.

MERLIN: (Pausing) So?

Giorgio turns to Merlin and smiles whilst raising one eyebrow. Out of his trouser pocket he produces a bright red apple.

GIORGIO: Behold! Here it is, I told you it's real. Didn't I say? Yes an apple, a bit like the old days from at least 50 years back … Well that's what it looks like, but this one is special. This one can live, grow and, dare I say it, even survive outdoors. I mean it. Outdoors! Not in a bio-tunnel or in a gas balanced poly tunnel, but actually OUTSIDE!

Giorgio's grin is now so wide it is starting to make him look unhinged, which matches with the far fetchedness of what he's just said to the man in white.

MERLIN: If what you say is true, you do know the implications of this?

GIORGIO: Of course. That's why the price is what it is.

MERLIN: Indeed, we've never heard of such a demand. A metre cube of solid pure gold. You should have gone for a full 20 tonnes, to make it even crazier. Madness, total madness! Why should I pay it? Why should my investors? Are you wasting my time?

GIORGIO: And yet you're here, aren't you? A full hour's robot ride through the fen.

It Means the World to Us

MERLIN: Okay, show me what I'm here for man.

Giorgio throws the red apple in the air and catches it triumphantly in his right hand.

GIORGIO: This apple is very, very special. It's got magical properties. You can grow it outdoors and …

Giorgio takes a bite, causing Merlin to try and fail to suppress a gasp.

GIORGIO: You can eat it.

MERLIN: I don't bel … But how? Aren't you going to, you know get the … The toxicity … I mean how can it be that you're not ingesting the chemicals? Why wouldn't it kill you?

Subconsciously Merlin looks down at his chemical monitor on his sleeve to check his exposure reading is still in the green.

GIORGIO: Oh yes. The killing you thing. Ha! I finally found a way to engineer a fruit plant to expunge, so to speak, the carbon fluorine chemicals.

MERLIN: How's that even possible? They're everywhere.

GIORGIO: Well the key is to accept that. You see the world wasted years trying to get rid of those fluorine forever chemicals, and well … You can't. I realised that I should do the opposite, don't fight nature, so I made a plant that absorbed it completely and then concentrated it. Rather than cyanide in the apple seeds, they've got all the carbon fluorine. And I mean all of it. There's nothing in the flesh, nothing in the skin, you can eat all the fruit, but the seeds are so toxic it'd kill an elephant.

MERLIN: Well it might do if they existed anymore.

The Apple

GIORGIO: Yes. The point is all the chemicals get concentrated in the part you don't eat. Which means we finally have a foodstuff we can grow outdoors again.

MERLIN: How does it reproduce?

GIORGIO: Well the seeds are sterile but that's fine as we take grafts, and those grafts are exact copies of the trees. They make exactly the same perfect apples, with the exact same perfectly poisoned carbon fluoride-riddled seeds, each and every time. You just throw them away and they're even in a little seed pod inside.

Giorgio hacks the rest of the apple apart, showing Merlin the apple seeds which are safely encased in a transparent seed pod.

MERLIN: Give me that apple. I want to analyse it.

The farmer hands over what's left of the red fruit to Merlin, who places some of the flesh of the fruit in a small digital reader. He immediately projects the findings onto his eye using the green output.

MERLIN: I'll be ... You're telling the truth. Good God man!

GIORGIO: (Grinning again and speaking with emphasis) Of course I am.

MERLIN: So where's the facility, how many have you got? Where are the tunnels?

GIORGIO: Look behind me.

Merlin stares uncomprehendingly for a moment, shakes his head and then points.

It Means the World to Us

MERLIN: What those? But they're outside. Trees outside. In the polluted air and soil. There's thousands of them, and they're outside. But ... But ... Of course, I see ...

GIORGIO: Yes, it's beautiful isn't it? You can grow them like trees used to grow, before the ... Well before it all happened. I've got them growing all over the Edge, all the way back down the hill for acres. Each one is a tree that can fruit. I've got three types of apple species to fertilise each other. Obviously they're all in the first pollination group so the blossoms don't get killed by the late spring heat ...

MERLIN: Can I go and look now? I need to see for myself. I'll give you a ride.

The robot horse slides under Merlin, lifting him on perfectly before replicating the move exactly on the second man. Merlin's cloak flicks out behind to maximise its surface area and suck in the sun's power. The horse heads without needing to be told, first along the Edge, then away past the old Druid's circle of stones, then on and back towards the lines of apple trees, which line down the slope of the hill and away from the sandstone cliffs.

GIORGIO: Here, grab one. Go and eat it, I'm serious, knock yourself out!

Merlin pulls at a large red apple. He tugs but it doesn't come off at first.

GIORGIO: You have to twist it and then pull.

Merlin does as he is told and picks an apple. He pauses for at least five seconds and contemplates the enormity of what he's about to do. Then he takes a bite. Then another large bite. He swallows.

The Apple

MERLIN: It's delicious. It's sweet and tastes so fresh, it's like something I read about as a child, descriptions that were in scanned books and internet footage back from the 21st century.

Merlin starts to cry. He is embarrassed but eventually regains his composure. Giorgio pats him on the shoulder and gets off the horse.

GIORGIO: I know. I get it. Three years ago when I realised it'd worked, I cried too. Like a baby. Then I got to work planting all these saplings and grafting onto some older trees. But I had to be sure it'd work. And it has. The trees can stay outdoors too because they just suck up the poison and it all goes straight into those apples. Then it goes into the seeds. Which means it's gets it out of the tree each and every year, and the tree can live out here.

MERLIN: I'll admit we didn't believe, or thought you were a crank. Personally I couldn't let myself believe it. I couldn't deal with the hope. (Pausing) You've got thousands here, there's enough to grow and graft a million or so in the first few years and then maybe a billion by 10 years after that.

GIORGIO: I realise. That's why a metre cube of gold is almost too little to ask. Crazy as it might seem. But I want this to change the world. Good God it needs it.

MERLIN: I'm taking some samples, but I'm sure now. I'm really sure. I know this is real. Humanity has finally got a way of growing food outside. It's a formality, so I can make the payment, it's not easy to source the gold, but we've got several of the councils of the world government to back us. One thing though …

GIORGIO: Yes?

It Means the World to Us

MERLIN: I really need to get indoors and away from the exposure, take a carbon powder shower and decontaminate. The usual.

GIORGIO: I'm sorry, where are my manners, let's go down, round the bottom of the cliff and I'll take you to my base. It's just at the shore there.

MERLIN: Sure, tell my steed the coordinates and we can go.

They get back on the horse after Merlin has loaded his samples into the storage areas. The analysis again confirms the lack of contamination in the apples. The horse takes them through the orchard and down to the Edge, then picks a path slowly down to the lakeside.

GIORGIO: Wait! It's here inside the cliff.

Giorgio taps his wrist communicator and two parts of the red stone shift apart to reveal a vast cave which almost instantaneously becomes brightly lit with a blueish light. This reveals a huge area of luminescent screens following the contours of the cave. Merlin's horse automatically goes inside carrying the two men inside the vast interior. The cave doors slide softly behind them.

GIORGIO: I'll make an arrangement for everything. I'm sorry about the excess security here, I needed some privacy and the cave is great for avoiding excess contaminants. Let's get the deal signed and block-chained forever. There is one more thing though?

MERLIN: Okay, I don't like surprises though, and the cave is … Unexpected. It reminds me of something.

The Apple

GIORGIO: Of course, it's nothing much, no concern but it's just that I really like your horse. It's not a deal breaker but after you've gone back on it, can you include it as part of the deal, and can you send it to come back with a reprogramme?

MERLIN: That's irregular but I can't exactly say no, which is a shame as I really like my horse. Still seems like karma, given what you've done for us all.

Merlin is distracted by something inside the cave, but there's nothing there to be seen, apart from the blue light and the high cavernous ceiling shaped of red stone.

MERLIN: Sorry, it's like I had a premonition or something. Like I'd been in this cave before, just a long time ago.

GIORGIO: I felt something. Like … Well, ancient. It flicked into my vision, weird. Lots of gold, lines of horses with people inside here. I must have it on the mind. Well we must be feeling the effects of being outside for too long, it can do strange things to the nervous system until you're clean. Let's go to the graphene shower and decontaminate.

MERLIN: One last thing. Can I take an apple for my daughter? She's young and has never seen anything grown outside. She thinks it's a myth.

GIORGIO: Yes you can. Take an apple. Paradise gained …

THE END